The Art Of Empathy

Poetries which Blossomed in Different
Shades of Life

DR. PALLAVI VIJENDRA SINGH

India | USA | UK

Dedication

To
The Noble Hearts,
My parents, My family & My Best Friends
To nurture my thoughts
and
Sculpturing my way of Expressions

Preface

"Understanding is an art", inherited in all living creatures. Animals express it in their acts but humans are fortunate enough to utter through their words. Understanding is required to strengthen an emotionally depressed heart, to uplift the disheartened hope, to share the slice of joy with an introvert mind. Eventually, the *Goal* is to mend the relations professionally or personally. How can this is be achieved? When situation slips through your tongue, take a pause, introspect yourself, you will find a reason of your plight.

"The Art of Empathy", is a book enclosing collection of poetry that bloomed in different circumstances of life. Every poetry unwraps a different story, depicting situations which knowing- unknowingly has been created socially, personally harming you morally. It gives a chance to precisely correct our relations. Some poems through empathy shows the beauty of relationships and good thoughts, some boost morally, some highlights the harsh face of society.

Empathy is your first step to make your life at ease. A heart ready to understand, will be a heart ready to rejuvenate healthy relations.

Remember Dear Readers,
"Your Art of Empathy hides answer to your questions,
 You are the only Arjun of your situations."

Happy Reading!!

(पद्मल्लव)
Dr. Pallavi V. Singh
Daughter of
Dr. Vijendra H. Singh & Smt. Savita V. Singh

Acknowledgements

My deep gratitude to my parents for *nurturing* good thoughts in me and eliminating negative aura within and around me, thereby teaching me *values of life.* I am grateful to my younger siblings for *sculpturing* and redirecting my opinion-based thoughts. Thank you to my concrete support, my best friends for stimulating a change in the *way of expressions* whenever thoughts lingered in same situation.

I acknowledge, **BookLeaf Publishing** team for coming up with the 21 days *Writing Challenge India* concept and creating new conceptual authors.

The only Sunshine

The only sunshine one hold,
that glitters more brightly than any grain of gold,

The one look that takes away all pain in tiresome day,
How any bud will blossom if sunshine taken away.

When sky is dark, so appears the bark,
This only smile, wipes thousand fear marks.

When with time only insecurity links,
When seeps of unfaithfulness any bond drinks,

The only face in eyes time brings,
Is this sunshine and with smile eyes blinks.

As fate said,
"Wrinkles, a day, petals will have",
but the roots will fulfil duties this word you have.

Learn to give First

May, parents be treated with loving care,
For their value is known only when we see
their empty chair;

Every leisure time with you they shared,
Sacrificed time, only to take your care;

In this struggle, grey turned their hair,
Now to move alone their shivering legs don't dare;

Pillars, they created once, now need to strengthen
their roof somewhere,
If demanded same, don't let your temper flare.

They never treated as if you were in orphanage,
So dear ones if you want a comfortable old age,

Learn to give parents the same,
Their teaching never allowed you to spoil their name.

Never treat them as if they are in old age home,
Remember, it was the same place they allowed you to
freely roam.

A Worthy Conversation

Once Almighty asked a roaming soul,
Oh Dear! Which birth you would like to have,
It smiled and excitedly replied- Dear Lord,

You can make me the stick to help a blind,
Or a flower to provide the nectar of its kind,

Or let me be the sword that will tear my countries foe,
Or the hope to make someone's life smoothly go,

Or a smile to make any heart happy with
non-verbal communication,
Or a pen to write the story of a revolution.

My Creator, please put me where I be best suited,
And He caringly replied- My Dear child,

Your chanted visions will have limited roles,
So, your birth will be as human, to achieve your multiple
goals;

The twinkling thoughts, started running smoother,
So, a happy soul was ready, to stress the nerves
and help out others.

The Unstained Thought

Pure love is divine, unstained,
Even if for a short span of time in your life it remained;

The hearts which cherish more the moments of
happiness,
Such good souls lessen the burden of emptiness;

When a life is blessed by such worthy gifts,
Your memories, from summer to spring it shifts;

These silk woven relations bring good fortune,
It doesn't matter, be they near or as far as moon;

The dream of strolling together by the beach,
they never keep,
Though remain far, in the gleam of moon light
Their true love peaks.

Till last breath pure sentiments never dies,

In many unheard thoughts such unstained story lies.

Hope never Dies

One who dares to smile alone in pain,
Will have guts to make all smile even in rain;

Be the torch and light your dimming flame,
Perform assiduously and win your game;

Dare to ignore the one who hurts you,
If time fails to learn what hurts you;

Live no life to entertain foes,
Who live in myth, let it be an answer to those;

Never let the hardship of life, make lose your smile,
If not on your lips, let it rest in the heart for a while;

Soon happy moments will retrieve as the time flips,
For sure, you will rejoice the moments you missed.

Conquering Hardship

One who dares to smile alone in pain,
Will have guts to make all smile even in rain;

Be the torch and light your dimming flame,
Perform assiduously and win your game;

Dare to ignore the one who hurts you,
If time fails to learn what hurts you;

Live no life to entertain foes,
Who live in myth, let it be an answer to those;

Never let the hardship of life, make lose your smile,
If not on your lips, let it rest in the heart for a while;

Soon happy moments will retrieve as the time flips,
For sure, you will rejoice the moments you missed.

A Banyan Tree

Never fear if you are facing any hardship,
if time is swinging violently its whip;

Something good is precipitating by deeds from you,
Soon your dream may come true,

or may be a discovery of new you,
which no peeking eyes earlier knew.

Dear all, faith your heart, close your eyes,
In your dark appeared fortune, a silver future lies;

Though with few or plenty of stings,
Don't let the wrinkles damage your wings;

In your strong believes let your soul take a dive,
Boldly immerge from your worry hive.

The Roar

I was sitting beside the door,
calmy enjoying my little cub's roar;

Days were going happily,
as he hopped around me merrily;

He loved, cared and even worries he shared,
forgot his injuries and made me happy in time he had;

Oh! Shockingly, good time takes more pause,
meantime weakens the relations with baseless cause;

His life still has the zest,
but smile brightens now only with the rest;

Once the eyes that waited for parental caring,
now allows only other voice for healing;

These waves crush my thoughts against rocky sea beds,
in his intentional ignorance my old age fades;

Still the trembling feet waited beside the door,
but the fragile cub started to leap long
and I lost his Roar;

Life acted as the dice,
With its last throw,
his fading smile took away my voice.

Why Crime goes High?

When kids do wrong and learn to lie,
The crime rate goes high.

When parents guard kids within security fencing
and anti-social ones teach how to cut those railings.
When good intentions are suffocated to die,
See, 'The crime rate goes high.'

When public start enjoying others screams
and innocents are made disabled to reach their dreams.
When cruelty conquers and loyalty die,
See, 'The crime rate goes high.'

When justice is beheaded by betrayer's saw
and violent mob rebels for impaired law.
When pleading voices are made to die,
See, 'The crime rate goes high.'

When respect for humanity burns in the fire,
the unheard protester still raises candle higher.

When politics make judiciary die,
See, 'The crime rate goes high.'

Flavouring the Favours

At the gate they picked you in arms,
When from school you reached soaked
in sweat charms,
Your tears they saw before rolling,
Your needs fulfilled before demanding.
This is *Parental Caring*.

At your murmuring sound notes they danced merrily,
Mentally were tired, still resolved
your problems happily,
Your act was treasured by them as talent,
Your stammering tongue was developed into an accent.
This is *Mentoring*.

They worked from light to twilight,
Struggling in dark hours to make your future bright,
Their journey with a blink moved from dawn to dusk,
Spreading fragrance of love stored as their musk.
This is *Self-enlightening*.

Don't let their shrinking eyes, see you flying away,
Their feeble feet can't resist till you return a day,
Their eyes will always be wanting for loved one's sight,
just repay their efforts and their sleepless night.
This is how you keep their *Lamp Illuminating*.

Innocence an Essence

Innocence is like an essence,
Love, care, politeness comes as its fragrance;

Tears of joy, give these qualities a feeling of
togetherness,
Innocent people love to give, but expects too less;

A person working for life tirelessly,
Is wanting for a heart who will care innocently;

Do cherish within the fragrance of innocence,
It can delay your life's senescence;

Cunning mind judges wrongly the heart of innocence,
Not everyone is fortunate to be blessed by this
inflorescence.

Quality Living

The standard of living,
must show standard of thinking,
empowered by parents teaching,
least must be concerned with standard of looking.

Soon your vision will be fogging,
your looks will be diminishing,
but with time, only you good deeds
like the sun will be dazzling.

It is awful to see an innocent heart,
trapped in a body with low art of living,
Dear ego mind, stop envying,
The return journey of your flock has been started,
just start living.

For monetary again, sacrificing morality,
Oh! Stop thy fooling.
Let life display your good heart, as time is running,
Wisdom is just chasing,

But your slippery words make your life derailing,

A kind heart will earn blessing,
A cunning heart will keep complaining.
You will earn what you are giving,
So, "let your standard of living
Reflect your standard of thinking".

Empowering Words

It can make you the king,
It can make you the pawn;
The power of your words stays,
even when you are gone.

It can give someone hope,
It can setback someone's dream;
The power of your words,
can connect hearts through an emotional gleam.

It can smoothen the hesitation,
It can build great warriors;
The power of your words,
can uproot any barriers.

It can humiliate a heart,
It can provoke to be a culprit;
The power of your words,
can flame the war and bring you guilt.

Illuminate the power of your teachings,
reflecting unconditional love of mother and father.
What a great victory!
when you make your home and society,
To live, a place safe and better.

Law of Growth

A young twig that appears delicate and fragile,
Teaches us to bend, to mend, when life makes you toil.

A River when it births, is drifted by tributaries,
See how, through its rise and fall,
goes with different identities.

Self-embraced bud, for once
hopes to crown the shoot,
Conquers the fear-
'Before blooming of falling' at the root.

The adult tree for decades sustaining storms,
Teaches to keep our roots deep and strong.

The one who inculcates a mind of traitorous,
your life repays by the same and
the outcome is enormous.

If you are strong to strangle some one's future,

your life will be ceased
failing your obscured morals to nurture.

Dauntless Dreams

Wings were wet, with edges curved,
The struggle for existence within genes it conserved;
Fluttered the wings with hope,
Solutions to the struggle it so far wrote.

The barrier it scribbled over its life,
the gossiping winds,
the taunting storms,
but the aim was strong like the scorching sun,
To rest a while after completing the run;
So, it fluttered wings with hope,
Solutions to the struggle it so far wrote.

Yes, a dream which never dies,
Time learns to crown a day
and the valiant heart dauntlessly flies.
This is the journey where...
Undisputedly it fluttered wings with hope,
Solutions to the struggle this is how it wrote.

The colour of success is bold and vibrant,
embracing all pains, all struggles within.
Answering all gossiping winds,
It ruled the air like a hind,
A change sprouted like the spring,
See, time wins.

Embracing Smile

Hopes may be shattered, in the fall of autumn,
or darkness may dwell at the heart's bottom,
though for a while,
but embrace your heart with a smile.

The strugglers are innumerable,
who morally fortitude in all situations
are very few,
Do embrace your heart with a smile,
The tide goes against or with you.

No longer will sustain, the erupting volcanic conflict,
when your tongue be stable
from plummeting in wrong situation, you will restrict.

The tide of time depicts
the fake world and facts of life,
some are slaves of fake addicts,
some struggles just to thrive.

Be the pillar, stop to blame,
like the wick just lit the flame,
no bad situation for long can remain,
be humble then for the sky you can aim.
"Though for a while,
Embrace your heart with a smile."

Introspecting Life

Life is about emerging from every wound,
reminding yourself not always to be frowned.

Without efforts don't expect to be crowned,
let the aura of affirmative people be around.

Filtering impurities, learning the art to give,
Life is about finding a new perspective to live.

Pruning away the splitting arguments,
and working on incisive settlements.

In life you can be the successor of success,
If creeping high after tumbling down,
you sight as adventurous.

Knitting Success

Don't expect to be valued!
Don't expect to be praised!
Then strong you have been raised.

But if you are valued,
If you are praised,
never fail to quote- 'It was a maze'.

The cunning minds from a distance will gaze,
let your eyes be aligned with your aim always.
Efforts when heated in furnace will let
the success glaze.

The success is not a position,
but a journey with different phases,
time rules and in different standards you get raised.
Some days, you win- you earn,
Other days, you lose- you learn.

Knitting success is an art of

learning, looping, knotting;
Keeping constant pace in your
agony, victory, calamity.
To earn a life of quality.

Unpredicted Life

Even a secured life can get suffocated to death,
or a rotten bud securely bloom in swaying twigs breath.

Even a fish may drown by its own water,
or a lifeless soul be drifted to the seaside and its
heartbeats flutter.

The Divine power that rests in our heart,
its aura is sufficient to save you from the poison dart.

Finding yourself after falling in agony,
is like crowned by time after a tragedy.

Life be like smiles filled in the hall,
or be like deep trench fall;

Till your edge is far you have to stroll,
Merrily except your every role.

Times Carves a Stable Heart

Autumn, be a fearful illusion,
again, you will sprout in the spring season.

Even if you are in pain,
Your prayers are sheltering someone in their rain.

No matter how much your feet shiver in cold,
Keep your path steady.

No matter how harsh the barbs come across your path,
Keep your speech steady.

No matter from within the scars make you speechless,
Keep your mind steady.

No matter if your mind suffers trauma,
Keep your faith on Lord steady.

The faith in the Lord can be shattered a day,
let your courage be steady.

No matter how many questions arise on your courage,
Keep your intentions steady.

Remember, when someone surprisingly gaze,
A smile should be steady on their face.

Shadow of Desire

A chilling night, I wrapped myself in a *Desire* shawl,
It gave my dreams, the warmth to crawl.

That night I got a sound sleep,
in dreams I was celebrating my future success leap.

The bursting applauses, the emotional gleam,
the sparkling honor was every heart's dream.

So easily success knocked the life it seemed.
Oh! But it turned to be like a daydream.

True! An effortless success, brings more distress.
The painful success is far away from regrets.

Let's make a watertight barrier,
in a daydreamer and achiever.

Beneath the shadow of desire lives a daydreamer,
With the flame of desire burns an achiever.

If you want to celebrate a place higher,
Don't quench the flame of desire.

www.ingramcontent.com/pod-product-compliance
Lightning Source LLC
La Vergne TN
LVHW010917200726
843509LV00013B/1974